SALES LANGUAGE
Rosie Victoria

ROSIE VICTORIA

To My Darling Daughter Luna -Rose,
Thank you for teaching me that love conquers all
X

ABOUT THE AUTHOR

Rosie Victoria is a leading Business Mentor for female Entrepreneurs all over the globe. She is the Women's Business Lounge creator, a leading brand that allows women to expand their wealth through Energy, marketing, and mindset training. She has a unique approach to sales and will enable you to break through your subconscious mind's barriers.

Rosie Victoria was Born in Yorkshire, England, in 1997 and rose to fame in 2017 when her Business began to get noticed. She runs a community of over 1000 individuals and hosts several digital programs per year to enable wealth acceleration.

www.rosievictoria.podia.com

wwww.instagram.com/rosievictoriax

Fb Group: Women's Business Lounge

This Book is copyright to Rosie Victoria Limited.

No part of this book must be reproduced, or stored in a retrieval system, or transmitted in any form or by any means, electronic, mechanical, photocopying, or otherwise without express permission from the publisher.

For permission request, please email rosievictoriacoaching@gmail.com

The Sales Language is a compelling, unique concept; this book provides you with personal knowledge but does not permit you to teach the sales language. All sales Language training must be booked through Rosie Victoria Limited. All love language credit to Gary Chapman.

Photography of cover: Becky Kerr @beckerrphotography

THE RECEPTIVE MOTOR

Sales are like a meaningless one night stand or the best love story of your life.

Sales is an art that requires us to be deeply in tune with our body's vessel; the minute we begin to throw away our intimacy for a quick temporary feel good is the minute we begin to feel all the wealth blockages. You can continue spending hours and hours searching for the perfect companion, or you can find yourself growing the most profound bond with yourself first so that you can receive all that you desire effortlessly.

Everything we receive in life comes from the receptive motor, a powerful mechanic which lives inside of our heart chakra and creates the circle of life in our reality. The motor operates in giving and receiving; the way we receive is through a divine balance of the push and the pull energies. Everything in life has a receptive motor, and sales are no different. If you desire to call in massive cash flow in your business, the energetic vibration of what you give has to feel in a relationship with what you want to receive. If you find yourself giving away more than you are receiving, you would need to check whether you are giving too much and creating an imbalance.

I know this all too well from the years I spent building a business wishing for wealth yet receiving debt. While my mouth said 'Debt Free,' my actions kept creating the codependent dynamic of scarcity.

I established my first business at the age of 16 in my mum's spare bedroom as a massage therapist, I was hungry for success, but everything in my energy screamed broke. I didn't understand the frequency of Money, and the power I dished to the universe portrayed a desperate reality. I would spend hours of my teenage years frantically searching for clients and committing to 12 hours of massage per day in the hope of wealth. Every client who came through the door felt like I had to drag them, and I was repeatedly underselling my services. My relationship with 'sales' was crippling my business.

Every time I would receive Money, the not-enoughness would step forward. I was locked in the cycle of needing sales; no matter how many clients I called in, the Money couldn't keep me afloat.

As a 16-year-old girl, I didn't have many overheads, but it didn't take me long to let this feeling of chase transition into reality. I was soon in a heavily abusive relationship, moved out of my parent's house, hustling harder, my debts were piling up, and sales began to feel like a massive chore in business.

My lack of understanding around Money meant I pushed out receptive energy lower than what I wanted to create. While freedom and wealth were on my mind, the truth is I had programmed my business for the chase.

When we are born into this life, we have no fears or understanding of Money. Everything we believe is passed down through subconscious programming. The human mind is programmed between 0-7, creating your life's views based on your guardians' influence. We piece together our perception of reality based on our peers' thoughts, feelings, and emotional responses.

Looking back now, the reason I chased sales is that it's all my receptive motor knew. I was yet to learn that our receptive motor could be reprogrammed at any point, so I was still clinging to the values which had been passed down from my parent's disappointment with wealth.

You can't turn your blinkers on to the very fact that your energy speaks to the universe before you do. You have to be prepared to change how you feed your energy out, or you'll always be in the cycle. It goes beyond the belief of changing 'how you think' and requires you to begin diving into your body's mechanics.

As I began to look beneath the surface of my own 'debt,' I saw that I was creating the belief that business was hard. Everything I put into my business was a reflection of the hardship I believed came with entrepreneurship.

Growing up, my dad ran his own business, which sacrificed all his time. He would work seven days a week and even then always claimed he was skint. You would see him scrapping for pennies in the shop despite having loads of notes, purely for the fact he was scared to spend them. My mother worked so hard but had to send us to childminders three days a week to work; she was always so tired when she came home that I just thought that was part of working life.

I continued reliving this story in every single aspect of my business. Everything from my advertisement to my sales conversations to my relationship with money repeated my peers' story.

The receptive energy alters when you allow yourself to take off layers of habit and allow yourself to become more abundantly connected with your work. The receptive state works via a response, and if you begin to respond to your business as a chore without any real meaning, then that's the energy you feed out.

In my days of debt, finances were a dreaded topic for me, and I lived every day in that energy. I would avoid my bills, I would feel confused in the organization of my wealth, and although I could receive sales, I wasn't entirely sure how to change my frequency, so I didn't repeat old habits.

Something had to change in my story of handling Money, or I would always be dishing out and receiving hot mess express.

What shifted for me was when I allowed myself to stop feeding my story of debt and desperation into existence.

I began to reeducate myself about what was expected from me if I wished to call in a high-level revenue. Suppose I would shift from the women in debt to the CEO bringing in multi-six figures; what would the leap look like? I couldn't continue being who I was right now, or I would continue to experience the same surroundings.

I became receptive to my four hundred thousand cash year by allowing myself to begin altering every inch of my being. I remember the question 'How would the million-dollar you share her energy with the world?' repeating in my mind every day with every action, thought, or story I played.

You can apply yourself to numerous external strategies, educations, and visibility hacks. Still, if your receptive motor does not feel compatible with what you're feeding out, then nothing is going to work. The key to balancing your receptive motor is to make sure every inch of your push and pull energies is the same. You are not giving nor receiving too much, and everything is a balanced frequency in your life.

Of course, it would be super easy to copy the successful women's push and pull energy, but unfortunately, we need to see that the real hack is by deepening the connection with self. Every single one of us has a different receptive motor. The frequency in which creates the circle of life will be different for each individual.

As a Leading Business Coach, I have been exploring the receptive motor for years, genuinely intrigued by what makes a successful business owner. It took me a long time to understand why there was no right or wrong answer to success. Success is not something we can follow a rule book on. Instead, it's deeply programmed in our body's mechanics: How you receive your sales is how you feel most connected.

You can carry on applying a million different ways to your business, but until you understand that you hold the most profound power, you will always feel like something is missing. Through learning to explore the body and sales, one thing that came to light is how we all love differently. The world wouldn't go round if we all had the same taste, and if you look beneath the surface of love, the foundation is different for each of us.

Some of us are sexual beings, and others are not. Some of us like time outdoors, some of us prefer time indoors. Some of us prefer more independence, where others desire lots of one on one time.

We all have different tastes, different connections with love, and feel whole in different scenarios. For me, I would be incredibly overbearing for some people. I need a lot of physical contact in my life; Sex, cuddles, kisses, etc. If I was to be with someone who couldn't provide those sparks in my life, what would begin to happen is that I wouldn't feel fully receptive. When we start to pull in the opposite of what makes us feel good, we don't feel satisfied. This creates enormous waves of disappointment in your receptive state.

We always say to women looking for love, 'don't settle for less,' but the saying should be, don't give out less.

What we give out is what we receive. If you are energetically sharing need and desperation, you will find a partner who continues aiding those feelings.

How you become receptive is how you feel receptive.

You can try to fit yourself into other boxes, but your body will only feel electricity connected with your mechanics. The mechanics, given to you at birth, will support you through every inch of your life if used correctly.

I would be lying if I said I had always listened to my body's receptive state; there have been numerous times where I have allowed situations, people, and strategies to get in the way of what feels right for me and my business.

There will always be times when we feel the disconnection; the difference is recognizing and responding accordingly. The minute you begin to feel frustrated with sales, the minute should start to assess how connected you feel with what you are pushing out into life form. Are you choosing lack of sales by not allowing pleasure into your purpose?

If you are not receiving what you want from your business, this is not that you are not capable but instead that you are not balanced in your divine push and pull. You right now are pulling in what is a vibrational match to what you are giving. If you are not satisfied, you must look at how you need to strengthen your wealth capacity first.

If you do not feel receptive in your life, the biggest question should be, 'How/ where do I not feel receptive in my life and business right now?'

Imposter syndrome is clinging to a state of energy that does not make you compatible with all you desire. Sales come from you being in tune with your body; we can only feel receptive when connected with our truth.

Looking at sales as a Push and Pull energy, this is where we must get in tune with our receptive state. If you desire to experience more leads, prospects, and cash flow in your business, then we must come home to your body's mechanics.

In my research, I was fascinated by how we all love differently, which confirmed that we all also sell differently. Our receptive energy doesn't change with what we are calling in. Whether you are manifesting-love, sales, or wealth, the receptive state must stay the same. If you feel electric, passion, and fulfillment first, then the universe will dish that back.

Where people go wrong in sales and love is that they try to change themselves. The belief that you have to do something different to receive is a limitation.

It instead has everything to do with how we feel when we are pushing our energy out into life. If you feel in Alignment, then the universe can grant your wishes.

You can not plan how you feed out your magic; it has to go through you and resonate with every inch of your knowing. Do you know that feeling where everything makes sense? It feels right, and you can't fight the urge? That's your knowing.

Tuning this into your sales energy, this is where you must allow yourself to channel your sense of knowing to receive. When you have that passion and most profound connection that something is right, the universe will hear you—stimulating the pullback from your powerful push in.

What you desire to call in can only be effortless and easy when you apply the same vibrational frequency to what you give. You can spend hours forcing what you give out to your business, but all that will create is receptive energy of hardship. If you want sales to happen rapidly without thinking about it, you have to allow yourself to hold that capacity first. Less time worrying about the sale and more time feeling connected to your offer or content.

I began to merge these two things into a potent formula…

Fuck ton of sales = Receptive state being activated by the body's pleasure and connection to work. A.k.a, you have to feel receptive first.

Love can either go one way or another, but the only way it feels good is when we have stepped into it for the right reasons and honored all of our boundaries first. Sales have to feel like love. If you don't want sales to cheat on you, take advantage, or make you chase, you have to realize that you are not for everyone.

If you saw your best friend trying to force herself into a relationship with a man who didn't see her, you'd be holding her back.

It would help if you now kept yourself back from showing up in your business with the same desperation.

You have a choice, you can either keep forcing things, or you can learn who you are, rise the fuck up and honor yourself. Meaning that Money can't stay away from you because you have an irresistible sense of truth.

Knowing and loving your truth is so underrated.

If you began to change yourself for love, you would find someone who didn't make you feel whole. Sales are the same. If you start to change your natural receptive state by applying strategies and beliefs that don't feel good for you, you call that back.

Sales get to be EASY when we follow this rule.

All you have to do is listen to what feels most receptive for you first. We can only receive what we are.

Below I have listed some incredible journal prompts to support you as you create your shift to wealth.

1) What sales energy feels right to me?

2) Does it feel natural to show up in this way?

3) Do I feel in love with how I am advertising or promoting myself right now?

4) What boundaries do I need when feeding out my sales energy so that I don't call in the wrong things?

5) Did my sales energy come naturally, or was it forced?

These questions are designed to help you recognize whether you are in your receptive state or not; this is something you can do whenever you feel blocked with clients or sales.

LOVE CONQUERS ALL

I now want us to travel deeper into how we love. How we love isn't something to be ignored; there's a reason why individual relationships in our life make us feel extremely receptive. I look back to the time I met Lewis, my partner; he allowed me to unlock the next level of wealth in my business. I had been navigating a shit storm of bad relationships because I always let my insecurities get the better of me.

It was a joke from the universe which took me a long time to understand. I kept opening myself up to less than I deserved in the hope of numbing the way I thought about myself. Lewis was the first healthy relationship I had because I did the work on myself. Summer of 2017, I began to see the self-sabotaging acts and acted.

By March 2018, I was madly, deeply in love with myself and my life. I walked away from a draining career, I ditched the drama of my on-off relationship, and I was doing everything I could to connect with my needs every day. The relationship didn't come because I needed it; it came because I had space for it. I was able to walk into a new partnership, claiming what I needed to feel loved.

I had learned that love could feel like a million flames of electricity or like your body was on fire, burning. There was no in-between.

We don't just wake up every day and feel loved by our partner; it's a constant feeding journey into pleasure. Each of us experiences joy on a different level, and we must listen to what feels right for us to activate long-lasting fulfillment. I stopped needing love because I was already creating pleasure in my life.

Whatever we desire to call in, we must fill the gap first.

If you desire more significant cash flow, sales, or more success, then you need to look at it through a lens of love. How are you not communicating your needs and standards? What must you articulate or push out to change the dynamic in front of you?

Throughout the next few sections, I aim to help you map out your unique sales energy. You are establishing what feels receptive and what feels icky to you. Remember, this is something that changes as we evolve as humans. We keep our relationship with sales evergreen by allowing ourselves to listen to our Alignment at the moment.

The Effortless Offering

First of all, the offerings in your business must come from the right place. If you allow yourself to force yourself to make money by trying too hard, the energy will come back tenfold. To create effortless offerings, we need to make sure you start from a pleasured state.

Sitting and wondering what's next is always taking your attention away from your alignment. If you have time to worry about whether people will buy or how to word things, then your attention is always disconnected from your pleasure.

This is where you must allow your offering to feel soul connected to you first. Rather than creating based on what you think others will buy, design based on what feels epic for your soul.

Look at love; for example, if you married someone just because you thought it was the right thing to do, later in life, you might feel disappointed realizing this person is not your match. When we put 'need' over our actual vibrations of fulfillment, the imbalance is created.

There is no right thing to do in sales or love. Instead, we must do what feels fantastic for our soul. You can't commit to something that doesn't feel equal in love.

Everything from pricing to services needs to feel soul connected.

Sticking with something just because your audience needs it is like committing to marriage because you think it's right.

Just allow your offering to come out of you effortless. Create at peace, and whenever you feel yourself drifting out of ease, this is time to take your attention away from the business.

The truth about money is that your intuition needs to handle the communication. When you allow your body to answer your business questions naturally, you will navigate to the right place.

I spent years wishing for wealth through my ego, and all it created was more frustration. Sales are not meant to feel hard but when we apply ourselves to selling when it doesn't feel right, that's what we create.

In December 2019, I kept trying to sell from my hospital bed. It was getting closer to the baby's arrival date, and fear was genuinely kicking in with how I would manage momma and business duties. I remember feeling like I needed to sell to stock up money. I was tired and exhausted, and the truth told, all I wanted to do was enter maternity leave. The more I showed up, the more I hit brick walls, and the more I got panicked. This is what Ego does. It makes you think you need to sell but, in reality, just creates more energetic blockages. In January, I finally admitted defeat, heading to the hospital again, I listened to my body, and I stopped for a while. At random points in the day, I would just start writing while waiting for my visitors.

I had no expectations. It flowed out of me, and the minute I wrote it down, I ditched any attachment. It was like a wave of channeling just swept through me into content with no effort at all. In February, Luna was born. In March, I had my first 32k cash week after beginning to share that random wizardry. I didn't have to sacrifice my time to make the sales come in. Everything happened without any effort.

When you use your body as the secret and let it show you the way, it will always honor your voice.

Money can't be the answer to your current problems. You have to ditch allowing your bills, current lack, and personal blockages to become a response to your business. The minute you speak from your pain (even if you think you had disguised it by pleasure), is the minute everything gets super icky.

For Example:

Linda creates an offer because she just got an unexpected bill that scared her; she made the offer based on what she thought people would buy. As a result, nobody signed up. She spent all day trying to get excited about the proposal but instead, felt lost and confused. The perfect thing for Linda to do here is to stop trying to sell and instead take herself away from the business. Linda could cook, go outside, have sex, do anything which stimulated pleasure. Later that day, Linda had a random idea for her business, which felt amazing. She didn't force it; it just came through. When Linda projected it, it created five instant sales.

Big Girl Business Energy

Big girl business energy is about looking at your capacity for wealth. If you desire more sales in your life, you have to level up your availability for wealth.

When we look at love, if you were continually allowing yourself to find love to avoid yourself, you would always call in a recipe for disaster. Nothing can fix us other than ourselves, and you have come to the wrong place if you think I will allow you to keep avoiding your relationship with money.

Looking at sales as something you always need doesn't feel abundant.

Big girl energy aims to create a system that requires us not to need to sell. When we look too deeply for love or sales, we often have to kiss many frogs before the prince. To cut the frogs out, then we need to change our expectations. Suppose you begin to play around with the confidence of people chasing you, eager to work with you, never settling for less than you deserve. Imagine the creation you would make.

How can you change your relationship with money so that you don't always feel called to sell? (Think here about your responsibilities, what bad habits do you keep repeating)

What money system will take off the pressure of always needing sales? (Think of pricing, payment plans, your savings, and business bank. How can you create a system which still has more than enough)

Are you creating right now because you feel called to do so or because you need to fix your money situation?

What boundaries do I need with sales so that I don't call in less than I desire?

REMOVING TRUTH BLOCKAGES

Allowing yourself to receive money is about seeing that you hold the capacity for everything. Many of us shy away from our wealth because we are scared to see what it might take. It takes nothing other than you choosing that you are enough. Once you hold the energetic vibration of settling for nothing less, money finds you irresistible. If you always find an excuse to be in lack, then you will continue living that story.

Below, I want you to Mind map why you believe money isn't available to you and ask what you need to do to release those beliefs.

LOVE VIBE

Sales are just like any other relationship; the energy must feel like an equal exchange for us to want to be there. This is where you need to look at what you crave from sales; if you are not fully satisfied right now, you are not building the energy exchange that lights you up.

FOR EXAMPLE:

I need to feel appreciated to feel balanced in love. I feel under-appreciated when my partner doesn't give me physical touch and communication. Reflecting this into my business, I know that to feel fully balanced as a businesswoman, I must feel this also.

Therefore, I must only make myself available to the people who can appreciate and support me. I should push boundaries for my work through pricing and personality, never sacrificing myself for less than I need to feel pleasure. When we understand that there is no shame in calling the shots on our needs and that our pleasure matters, we begin to break the relationship of overextending. We are receiving based on satisfaction, not autopilot.

As you combine all these practices, what you begin to do is choose love through sales. Recognizing that you feel receptive in a completely different way to those around you, you will start activating the receptive motor through choosing self and pleasure.

I now encourage you to go map out who you are before society programmed you to respond. You hold no fear or codependency to sales. You can create as lustfully and magnetically as you desire. What higher self are you pulling forward?

THE SALES LANGUAGE

The sales love Language is diverse teaching, which has been created by Rosie Victoria Limited, inspired by the love languages created by Gary Chapman in 1992. This teaching shows you how to allow your sales to feel receptive AF.

Our Love Language is home to how we feel appreciated, connected, and intimate with the partners in our life. To have healthy, strong bound connections, we must feel comfortable with receiving all that we need.

Gary's teachings are all about making your partner feel appreciated, but one thing I realized about sales is that it's not about our prospects. The more we try to tailor to our audience, the more limiting our messaging becomes. Instead, we must connect to what makes us feel good first. Taking the Language that sets our soul on fire, we can then use it to form our sales strategy.

What I created here is a direct hack to get into your body's receptive state. Taking the concept of the love languages created by Gary Chapman, what the Sales Love language does is show you how to feel infinitely bonded with your sales energy.

There is a reason why you only feel compatible with the people in your life who can feed into your Language. If you were trying to force your Language of quality time upon someone who didn't like one on one space, then you would always be reaching hiccups in the relationship. The sales Love Language allows you to attract your people by getting comfortable with what makes you feel receptive.

Someone who enjoys quality time needs quality time to receive quickly.

If we deny ourselves what makes us feel whole, we will always feel something is missing in our sales and business. We are usually good at giving the service we want to receive, and actually, this balances the push and pull energies.

QUALITY TIME

Those who have a language of Quality Time need to have uninterrupted attention. How they feel receptive is by being locked in the moment of bonding. If they think someone's attention is drifting elsewhere, they begin to feel like they are not being seen. It's essential for the women who need quality time to schedule one-on-one time in their schedule.

Now, if you vibe with Quality Time, then your sales energy also needs quality time.

You are not someone who can throw out a sales link and hope for the best; you are a soul who needs to feel infinitely bonded.

For you to generate maximum clients in your business, you have to allow time for quality bonding. What is essential for the sales energy here is that you allow yourself to spend time nurturing relationships in a one on one setting. It is heavily vital for Quality Time Women to make bonding a massive part of her sales energy;

she must feel able to communicate her sales power without attention drifting elsewhere.

A few things that will activate the Quality Time Women:

-Sales call to build relationships, be in the moment, and showcase magic.

-Spend time building relationships in a one-on-one setting, no generic bullshit.

- Spend time nurturing offers. Get intimate with your ideas and continue to evolve them before projecting them to the world. (you will create better launches by having a date night with your projects)

-Being in a present environment with clients will help magnetize the soul connection. It would help if you felt involved in the moment.

ACTS OF SERVICE

The Acts of Service woman appreciates the small appreciation of receiving acts of kindness. She feels most loved when someone can contribute to her day by thinking about her through services. She is a thoughtful soul who feels most receptive when she is thinking of others and vice versa.

The act of servicewomen feels under-appreciated when she is doing everything on her own. It feels good to release the burdens. It is heavily essential for servicewomen to have a strong team in their corner.

The little things are what she loves to give, and those of you who love acts of service should be looking at sprinkling some random kindness into your community.

A few things that will activate the Act Of Service Women:

- Hiring a team and allowing others to take off a load of service, also hiring a team who can think about what she needs before she does (GAME-CHANGING)

- It feels most connected when answering a solution. The servicewomen will be able to see what her client or surrounding needs and create accordingly—diving into the energy of making a difference.

- Your audience will want your help, so you need to be ready not just to tell them but offer to help them through each step.

-Allow your prospects to fuss over you, they need to be ready for your magic, and it feels good when they contribute appreciation. Almost let people dedicate their charm to you before you commit to serving them.

RECEIVING GIFTS

The receiving gift women love thoughtfulness; it's not necessarily about the gift itself but instead the energy exchange. Are you someone who loves to buy gifts and finds great pleasure in treating those around you? If so, then this is your pleasure zone.

The receiving woman needs to be highly connected with everything she gifts out; to her, it's the gesture that means something.

If you like to receive gifts, then it's time to start giving to your audience.

- Think about perfect gifts that help them feel into your energy. What can you give that allows them to experience you before investment.

- The warm up stage is essential; you only feel receptive when you know you are giving.

- Think of slowing down the process and providing lots of magic first. If you gift others your magic, they will bless you with wealth.

PHYSICAL TOUCH

We love to experience nonverbal contact with those around us for those who feel receptive through Physical touch. This can feel hard to transmit in our sales energy because we can't kiss, hug, and physically connect with our prospects.

It is much easier for us to be in front of individuals rather than behind a computer screen. You will find yourself seeking in-person communication and be lit up by hands-on work: Massage therapy, healing work requiring hands, or any in-person job role.

A few things that will activate sales for the physical touch women:

- Radiate sales energy through physical contact. Lock the sale in person, handshake, or ask what physical contact could represent online...

Example: You need physical touch to feel receptive. How can I reflect the energies transferred through physical contact in the online space?

- Look at hosting in-person retreats or events.

-Work with clients in the same room.

- Allow yourself to share physical touch in your content, advertisement, and marketing; reflect on how you can replicate the emotional exchange of physical touch.

WORDS OF AFFIRMATION

It is heavily important for the word of affirmation to be relatable to where she is. She can only sell when she is raw, open, and allows herself to vocalize her voice's deepness. Words of affirmation women will feel receptive when she receives random compliments or has an engaging conversation. Her audience needs her words. They need her to tell them the journey through her choice of words.

Activating sales through word of affirmation:

- Clearing and removing throat chakra blockages

- Allowing yourself to focus detail on the wording of offers or launches

-The Language of your advertisement means everything. Be comfortable telling the tale. Spend time taking people through your journey with words/steps into other people's emotional engagement.

How to know which love language you are?

Knowing which love Language you are is about recognizing what makes you feel whole; what do you need to feel fully loved and appreciated in life? When we allow ourselves to take the formula of what makes us feel receptive and apply it to sales, this is when we magnetize easily.

Sales should always be a simple extension of being what we love; it doesn't matter how much you do; if your soul does not feel connected, appreciated, and understood, then the energetic frequency will be all wrong.

Connecting to your sales Language is about coming home to your natural body, you as the leader, gets to claim what feels good. The age of wealth being about sacrificing our soul to the hustle is dying, and it's time to allow it to be easier.

XOXO

Rosie Victoria

The Sales Language is a very detailed Live program that launches in February of 2020. This is a practice that can only be taught by Rosie Victoria Limited. See copyright details.

This 12-week program will allow you to anchor into your unique sales language as a way to call in more sales in your business.

For details on the program, email
rosievictoriacoaching@gmail.com

Gary Chapman created the Love Languages, and all credit must be given when referencing his work. The sales Language is a unique training created by Rosie Victoria Limited, backed by studies and research to help you understand your receptive motor. You are not legally permitted to teach the Sales Langauge unless granted permission via Rosie Victoria.

To discuss permission, please email.

SALES GET TO BE EASY
SALES GET TO BE FUN
SALES GET TO BE PLAYFUL

www.ingramcontent.com/pod-product-compliance
Lightning Source LLC
Chambersburg PA
CBHW070912220526
45466CB00005B/2201